RINSE

RINSE

Elaine Terranova

Grid Books BOSTON

GRID BOOKS
Boston, Massachusetts
grid-books.org

COVER
Cliff in Shadow, 2020
Susan Migliore
Oil on canvas
8 × 10 inches

Printed by McNaughton & Gunn
Saline, Michigan

ISBN: 978-1-946830-17-3

To Lee, always

CONTENTS

5. SPIN

Short Memoirs of Life on Earth

I grew up in a house
where there was no money for anything but food
and maybe orthopedic shoes

At night I lay curled like a pearl, a ball shaped
by nacreous limbs. I might have unpeeled
from night from sleep from my covers
in surprise, like a passenger stepping out of a car

*

My mother called my father Nussie, little nut.
No one else did. I called him Dad, and as a child,
in my unintentionally childish way, Daddy

—When my brothers weren't there
somehow the heart went out of the house—

How awful I felt when I found out
the rabbit didn't volunteer
the lucky foot on my key chain

*

On my own, I lived once four floors up
from a subway so that I woke, shaking

There, I was never sure music
was knocking at my door. I thought what I heard
might be meant for somebody else

*

Instead of getting down from the shelf each night
four various dental flosses for cleaning
the four variously spaced openings between my teeth,
I see I can get down just two at a time
to make this an entirely new experience

*

So much of the day I am ashamed of what I've done.
I can't forgive myself.
Until I am ready to go to sleep and realize
I have by then forgiven myself
for a dozen additional offenses

*

Red, the tooth-torn berry I once saw
in my path through the woods. I hope it satisfied

Red, the tiny, exact mushrooms
like spots of blood I came upon farther on

*

—It seems I can't think one thought without
an earlier one shining through—

*

A river ran past
that hunting lodge in Wyoming

All night it lay quietly beside me and in the morning
showed itself, moving faster than I could move,
dividing me from the world

*

In Rome, at Largo de Torre Argentina
ruins awaited me
but also a shelter for cats

A huge silver moon filled the sky
and spilled over onto our faces

*

Oh, Earth! During the recent eclipse
how naked you seemed without your star.
I feared if the sun collapsed
you'd only grow colder, harder, darker

yet new stars are born all the time
in clusters, like litters of kittens

1. WATER LEVEL

Aubade

Sad silver light,
the opening light of day
launching me
into the bewilderment
of morning

though now at least
I can speak.
I am no longer seated
in the quiet car of life

or lizard-like
slithering
through a dream
with no accompaniment
but the jolt of my pulse

outside, only
the questioning cries of birds

later I will find
my place in the landscape,
get to that catch in the road
where water falls,
that catch in my throat

then it could be
a small animal
even an insect I spot
quivering in the grass
or just the face of the wind
showing itself
the only way it knows how

Tan Espadrilles

I am scarcely pedaling, the wind is carrying me off on my bike. Down the wide avenue. I detect a whiff of salt in the air, shore air. Tan espadrilles are light on my feet below beige linen trousers. A light shirt over my t-shirt flies out to the sides in the breeze I am making. I am propelled by sunlight, following you, weaving in and out of cars in the light traffic that edges the street. You are before me, showing the way. I try to catch up, with my loopy, less powerful legs. The bike and I are one fantastical creature, a hybrid, a female centaur. If I am any lighter, I will dissolve. Maybe we are back in Ocean City after so many years, islanded by water, nothing familiar, free to appear or disappear. Or I am lifting off into the sky of my childhood, in Logan, all the shops going by, the kosher butcher, the fishman, the bakery that makes creampuffs and strudels. But when I look for you, after you, you are gone. I turn off where I thought I saw you turn off, into a narrow, shaded street in Italy or California, and lean the bike against the white-framed, plate glass window of a pizzeria. I wander in and the men in white aprons are taking a smoke, slouched in wooden chairs, wreathed in clouds of smoke or flour as they wait for the wood burning ovens to be ready. But I ask and they haven't seen you. I go back out and, reunited with my bike, don't know whether to keep riding and leave to chance my hope to catch up with you somewhere or turn around.

Monkfish, Manatee

Monkfish, that looks to be more human than other fish. More human except for maybe the manatee which isn't even a fish but a mammal trapped in water and we don't anyhow eat them. Oh, I'm so happy I don't need to clean or cook it today, monkfish, fillet the texture and shape of our guts, with its thin, slippery membrane that should be pulled back and over like a pair of socks rolled into a ball. Though the membrane breaks down and melts in high or prolonged heat. When done, it could be any other fish even if tough and resistant un- or undercooked. I once saw a manatee rising from the shallow, dirty water edging Tampa Bay. It floated amid chip bags and popsicle sticks like a swollen baby. I can only imagine a monkfish alive, with its wide mouth. Both it and the manatee, with their similar bewildered, homely-man faces.

Mom-in-a-Box

I placed my mother in a box, white cardboard for instance as if for takeout Chinese. She's packed away like dime store dolls we sent to displaced children in camps after the war when I was in third grade, along with little accoutrements, toy tea sets and dollhouse furniture. They nestled like pharaohs traveling with grave goods into eternity, dogs and jewels they had in life. My mother didn't want to stay but I made her, folding her arms across her chest and tucking in her apron. I fitted tabs in slots and threaded through a thin wire so she could be picked up and carried away, with space for my four fingers.

Mirror

I call her from our cabin in the woods. She says to me, isn't that funny? she's in the woods too. "It's all green outside. The kids have treated me to a holiday," she thinks, because they are like that. "Always doing funny things for me that will make me happy."

Can she go swimming where she is? Has she met the other people there?

"I've only been here maybe four days!" she tells me, so I don't think she's had all the time in the world.

She thinks the place is in Florida but in a strange part, maybe far away from where she lives. I ask if she got there by train. By car, maybe?

"Oh, it must have been car. But I don't know who drove me. (Isn't that funny?) They even brought my sofa. And I see all my books on a shelf. And some writing paper too," things to make her feel at home.

"But they can't have meant me to stay. I'll call them and find out where I am."

"What do you do with yourself there every day?" I ask.

"What do you do where you are?"

"I take walks, hikes, really. Because it's pretty hilly."

"Me too! Do you wear hiking boots? I do, but they're a little tight so they pinch."

"That's not good," I agree. "And they are also very heavy."

"Mine too! I'll have to get a new, light pair if I stay here. Oh, I just looked in the kitchen and they even thought to bring my kitchen table so I can make dinner. Isn't that nice?"

World Written

My hand cramps now to fit the words between notebook lines where they are intended to nestle. But what if there were no lines, the whole world an empty blank I am free to enter anywhere?

I have been reading after I wake in the night. I close my eyes and open them again and a fine line of type is imprinted on the red-orange inside of my eyelid: *080873* it reads, like a password. Or "Chloe," someone's name. Or maybe what I see is the mandate, *chase*, or *chase it*.

Overheard

Oh, the allure of distant music. It transcends space even if I am not its intended recipient. Found music, its point worn down in passing. The run of notes followed avidly but from a distance. I am not overcome. It does its business and is gone, like a whispered conversation at the door of another room. Or the wind or the sea. It is without obvious agency, not self-conscious. Inexact. I am not devastated by the silence that follows.

Tomato Man

I see the Tomato Man, whose stand we stop at Sundays for the plump, ripe globes, flesh the color and sweetness of roses, he has nurtured through the spring. Sometimes though, all he has left are tiny and shriveled, lopsided like pouches of seeds but we buy them anyway.

Today I am surprised to find him separate from the wooden lean-to adorned with pennants and flags the wind whips to attract customers. Instead, he has driven his rickety tractor out into the world. A torn American flag waves from a pole connected to a fender. He is tired of waiting for us to stop and is far now from his little farm, really the backyard behind a trailer. Goggles or a gas mask or some other disguising device obscures his features. He may not want it to be known that he isn't around at his stand to take our money, fearing tomato thieves. He drives like a teenage hot-rodder, not the octogenarian he surely is.

Soon he is far from his plants and circles into a gravel-topped parking lot. We follow as he dismounts and enters the cinderbox building that is his destination. We take seats before him where he stands at the front of the auditorium before a chalkboard. The Tomato Man, a motivational speaker, scribbles on it something indecipherable and begins his talk, his voice and a hologram of his person bouncing around the room electronically so fast and disconnected we have trouble taking notes.

A.C.

When I swung by in a car along the avenue, or walked down the ramp from the boardwalk onto an unknown street, I saw how people, even people who had houses, lived outside on the sidewalk those warm summer evenings in Atlantic City. They faced the sky, sprawled in beach chairs set out beneath the moon. Babies sat in laps in the living room light spilling out from open windows. Grown-ups ate their supper and drank cool, effervescent drinks that bubbled up in a rainbow of colors, and read the paper. I never forgot I didn't belong and savored the cool wind of my solitary incursion.

Peace

That he found such safety in a house, my nephew, I was glad to know. That the murmur of parents in the bedroom beside him soothed like the sound of the sea and he could finally let himself go, enter the dark passageway of sleep. Oh, it was something to envy. Something I had not experienced, kept up by my own parents' noisy squabbles. Even grown, my nephew said, he loved to spend the night at a married friend's, a house sanctified with a couple's sleep, especially where children lay near, tucked up in bed. And he told me about his night by the shore, at Jake's. So at peace, my nephew slept well into the morning of the next day, waking with the box of the ocean swinging toward him and away like the gulp of a first word he woke with in his mouth waiting to say. But no one was anywhere near. When he rose from the couch where he'd slept, the blinds were still drawn. He heard nothing, not the noise of TV or cries of a child finding itself suddenly alone in the day. They've all gone out, he decided. But the dishes lay stacked in the sink and wineglasses etched circles on the coffee table beside him where they'd been set down the night before. So eerie, so silent, it seemed to him after a while that something might truly be wrong. Maybe the gas had leaked from a pipeline and they all lay dead in their bedrooms above. He sat alone on the couch, not knowing what to do, when in the next half hour, his friend and his wife and the two little girls all drifted down to him, one by one. You should write this in a story, I told him. No, he said. I'd need to make it more interesting. To be a story, I'd have to say that they had all really died.

2. ON

X

I have the feeling that I have misplaced something. I know, my ex-husband from some forty years ago. Or the baby I forgot to have.

But you couldn't exactly forget a baby. How with a baby, you would need to keep it in yourself a whole three-quarters of a year, then on yourself affixed to the breast, then by your side at least, linking fingers. It's that precious. Even if you might imagine putting it in a drawer you don't look in again.

And was the name of the baby to be Bruno? Or was that the dog?

The Songbird's Mate

Song, which differs from call. Song, in some cases, a poor effort. Tumble of notes. Done for its own sake or to win a mate. This I knew by experience or instinct.

What to make of the stillness then. It smelled of him. It smelled his way but didn't allow for movement. What had death done exactly? Bent a wing, and there was no voice. His voice that was different from others', smooth, winning, perfectly projected. No voice to say, "No. Stay put till it's safe." And it took the shine out of the alert eye.

Death is lying in the road. And I, each time go forward, only to be cut off by a car. Car approaching, surely that's death. Then is death what happens or what it happens to? Lying in the road is death. I go forward, I come back. I go forward and startle with the breath of an approaching car. I rise. I fly to the opposite side of the road. Up to a tree or a telephone wire. Day continues, rain and spring. That is not death, but the flat, empty shape in the middle of the road, that's death.

Sky. Flap of wings. It's light and then it's dark. Off, I fly off at last. Death isn't careful, doesn't care. Death doesn't have a preference.

Out of the Past

When the train cut through the tunnel, everything changed
due to darkness and sudden pressure. The molecules of air
solidified. Did no one notice? Maybe they took it for granted
as they did that we were no longer moving and stood still as
the egrets in rushes pinning down the curve of New Jersey.
My head fell to the shoulder beside me. My hand tightened on
his hand. But I knew any minute we'd surface and be safe, the
two towers appear, entrance to the city. Always the towers at
the face of the horizon, you depended on them, gate of horn
and gate of ivory, telling whether to believe or disbelieve the
dream.

Angel, Sleep

There was a beach and an apartment house on the beach, the house called Angel, or Sleep. I had come to it invited, if not by a friend, then an intimate acquaintance. I was offered no towel or blanket to put under me, no ready chair. I settled into the yellow sand and the sand gave way. I displaced it with the expanse of my body. This was not pristine white beach, the beach of my childhood. Only workaday sand shored up for playgrounds and worksites where now men in long pants were playing tennis or painting green a wall that shut us off from the sea, a view you didn't take for granted, you couldn't exactly believe was there.

Then someone was running toward me in the sand, the slightly muddy sand, his feet exacting speed from it. Past the sunstruck crowds. He was just hitting his stride as a lover, the thunder of that eagerness.

Before the Trip

I'm neither here nor there, still casualty of the 50-mile wind gusts the day before, the sprays of rain that blew me over. I clung to the bus shelter but nothing was coming only water and wind. A vertigo gripped me. I couldn't tell up from down. My head beat with the clatter of outdoors. No wonder then today to find myself indecisive over a bowl of udon. The noodles go one way; they go another. They cannot be pinned down. I slurp, slurp, as I've seen people do in Japan. Their only weapon a ceramic spoon, but I grip silverware, fork and tablespoon, with the same tenacity I used in yesterday's gale. I've tied a paper napkin around my neck like a ruff. This they do in Japan as well, to protect against the long, thick noodles flailing every which way, so instead they may be drawn sleekly into the perfect round openings of their mouths.

737

Soon I will lap the country, dividing it in two designated stretches. But planes are going down. The cones of their noses, specially designed to point up, up, into the sky to reach a flying level, now only turn downward as gravity or the change in time flips them over.

Morning Housework

Straightening the bed, smoothing the sheets around my form. Then I rise and with a bouquet of feathers, do my little dust ballet.

Outside

That's what it's called. Where the ground shines, wet with early morning mizzle, which is mist and drizzle. The house across fronted through the night by a single wavy bulb flickering like gaslight or the beacon of a lighthouse, so someone will know to come.

Replacement

What if the knee doesn't take to me? If it's at odds with my body and strikes out in a whole new direction? If, in fact, it has a metal mind of its own. Then it may take me someplace I do not want to go. I wonder how it kicks, built as it is like one wing of a nutcracker. Also, how I refer to it, née—what? Does it have a maiden name? And its upkeep which could be expensive, and may, for instance, require a stationary bicycle for exercise. The rest of my leg has already moved aside a little above and below, making room for it. What could I do about that?

3. PERMANENT PRESS

Laugh Track

I was dismayed to realize that no one in our household listened to me, seemed to hear a word I said. In fact, it was best, most efficient, oftenest that no one listened to anyone but sat with a kind of reverence, their attention directed to the radio. And the way recorded laughter punctuated a show, a laugh track might have been affixed to our lives. My father, for instance, guffawed deeply once or twice, cracked the air, really, with something like a sharp bark. Scary, how he laughed. You wanted him to, companionable, but also scary and were kind of glad if he didn't do it again. On the other hand, no out-loud sound ever escaped my mother. Her belly maybe shook as if she was afraid, as she warned, her sides were splitting. My brothers, Leo, Sidney: Leo sucked air in to laugh but not all of it came out. It could sound sometimes like strangling. And Sidney, his laugh was a little, snuffled breath repeated over and over through the nose, or a nervous giggle, self-conscious, like clearing his throat. Sometimes I imagined it sounded like Richard Widmark's, throwing the old woman down the stairs in the movie.

Er Lakht

That would be my father
at the fireworks in Fairmount Park
on July 4. It is only two days since
his birthday. The display, as if meant
for him, close by the spigots where
we sometimes come to fill our gallons.

Er lakht, my mother says,
for indeed he is pleased, laughing
to himself, standing on the floor
of colors where they have landed
from the lightened sky. My mother,
who fears crowds and loud noises
and the smoke of brightness.

And I, what was I to make of it,
night going to color, fingers of fire
that bid and then withdrew?
Night hovering, liquid jewels
erupting, red, green, blue,
even a waterfall of silver as when
in hottest summer, with other children,
I went under the hose a mother held,
spray first, then a notch up to needles.

Now I crawl through a fence of legs
to see. So brilliant, the work
of these fire specialists
who want us to love them. At the end

I am breathless as mad, cascading shapes,
pound down on us uncontrollably
like the spears of gods.

How gentle, then, my father's laugh
in comparison. When he bends
toward me, *er lakht*, he's chuckling,
as his love comes down
to me in little gorgeous pieces.

Overcoat Dream

Sad, evening. How can I get to tomorrow? Is that with two m's or two r's? Two m's would be odder. Oder? Isn't that "other" or "or" in German? (Maybe "but"?) The only path to tomorrow is sleep and sleep is a terrifying prospect. What waits inside it but dreams? Even worse if sleep were to be empty. But should there be a dream, for instance, my father in hat and tweed overcoat. His tortoiseshell glasses. The hat at a jaunty gangster tilt onto one side of his forehead (he has always borne a resemblance to Edward G. Robinson). "Did you hear the bell? Don't you know what you're doing? Chrissakes! Answer the door!" he shouts at my brother Sidney who is coming down the stairs in his National Guard uniform. Sidney, with an unexpected, long reddish beard. Though my father never in real life has said a mean word to Sidney. Why did we not call my brother, even refer to him, as Sid? His friends did. Just the two of them, my father and my brother, in the house. In perpendicularity. And maybe it's me at the door, come to witness. The last time I saw my father was at his funeral. "That's not my father!" I cried. It didn't seem to be. Maybe I looked around, hoping to find him standing at my side. In the dream he is sitting or lying down, the tent of the overcoat, voluminous, has dropped from above, settling over him like his life. I can't get accustomed to the dark. My knee aches, and my shoulder. I see I am to be locked in the dream's room, just me, alone.

Cactuses

I look out past the cluster of miniatures, gregarious, a family: father cactus, mammillaria, hen and chicks. Like other families, they don't mean to hurt one another. Little tender cactuses roughhousing. Contiguous, touching, fixed in their small cement garden. Hair like thistle, like needles. They stick each other. One, a redcap, is blooming a strawberry like a bleed. Indoor planted, poking collectively, the hedgehog, the fish hook. Sweet to see though a danger to one another, to a passing hand. If one should fail, the others lean to it in the pot, solicitous, suffocating, as if to ease its suffering.

Case

"I had to, like, open the bruise up and let some of the bruise blood come out to show them." —Daniel Hamm, a young Black man, making public his beating by the police

"Come out," he said, when he cut the bruise open to show the TV and newspapers. Only the encasement of skin between blood and outside. If breached, blood would spill. He saw he was, like us all, a sack of blood. Look at our faces, the obvious spigots, eyes, nose, mouth, when a blow is struck or a vital organ perhaps explodes. The whole point of us is blood, its unobstructed flow, except for the barrier of skin. Even in the safety of a house, a sink could fill with it, the clawfooted tub overflow. The whole container of the bathroom, with its jutting white enamel fixtures, a potential box of blood.

Heat Death

1. One day everything will be the same temperature and no work get done.

2. The present, I've learned, doesn't really exist, or if it does, just briefly, pressed as it is against a black hole of forgetting.

3. And marriage: Is it only whispers behind the window shade?

4. I could never do enough for him, even with the exaggeration of my Jungle Gardenia perfume. How enticing it must have been, to imagine a life without me.

5. And so, entropy, heat death. When we left the mountain, time accelerated as if drawn down by gravity, eager to reach bottom. We rode into the sun along Armand Hammer Boulevard. Arm & Hammer, I pictured the bent elbow on the baking soda. "Slow down!" I cried. The brilliant Colorado light unnerved me. "Christ, it was only beer!" he shouted, for I'd noted he had been drinking. At the bottom of the sky he speeded up and the car struck out, independent, driving up on the slant like a bridge opening.

6. We used to be those people, then we stopped being them.

Islets

I opened my front door, inches, perhaps a foot, to witness the arrival of first snow. Quite beautiful, how it fringed our tiny street, the Arts and Crafts houses. Then, though I struggled with the heavy wooden frame, obstinate as a tree, pulled and pulled with all my dream might to draw the door closed, my hands had no force. I looked down at the small coals, some of them live, that had wedged themselves between inside and out. The warmth of the house was escaping as I stood, trying to withdraw, while in the street phalanxes of young people massed before me in strict formation. Where they were was a whole other weather system, sunny and clear, I was sure, "Look how they are dressed," though my eyes couldn't find the sky through the solid density of bodies. I called out, "Where is your home?" and a girl turned. "The Islets of Langerhans," she said. I'd never been. It must be paradise. Sometime I should go, I thought.

It's Snowing

It's snowing so hard, with all its might. I and others on our street are rosy cheeked, in layers of clothes, in stocking caps that melt over our shoulders like frozen custard. And mittens. On the sidewalk in the snow, shoveling, playing like children. We are so small in this weather. But there's a cast of shadow too and a heaviness then, grey, almost the shade of ice. People have fashioned tunnels and igloos with the soft snow that will harden into shape. So much snow, so much winter. A car comes along, people I might know. A couple I can't find the names for. "Come with," they say and open the door. And off we go around the block to the backs of the houses, and I see they are falling down, propped up by wood posts that reach up almost to the second floor. Here, the houses are drenched in sunlight, the snow, practically gone. The upper story has windows and little porches like pockets. On one, a basin the shape of a fur muff rests on a table. A man is looking out at the pair of birds nestled in it like praying hands. Grey mourning doves. I see the houses in a different light than I ever did, in primitive colors, green and red, yellow. So this is the back side, I think, the back of what I've only faced from the front. And I know I'm seeing what I shouldn't be able to from a car below, the inside of it still in winter. I get out. I want to be faithful to the true color I remember in movies, True Color, it's called. The scene, like someone in a comedy who turns around, the back of her clothes peeled back to bloomers.

Shaking

Things shaken to let out the last reluctant drop:
From a tiny, self-administering bottle, doses of sunshine,
    liquid vitamin D.
My miniature LED flashlight, emitting intermittent, erratic
    licks of light.
From the male organ, a pearl of what passes.

Flute

I follow the shrill, melodic passages from the moment I shut
my door. I follow, glancing at each house I pass, sure it must
be harboring a practicing student, since my path takes me
past the Institute of Music and this is where a young flutist
might be stashed in some basement apartment. Oh, I go for
blocks like this, enticed, like a rat or a child. When the Square
appears I enter it. The sound swelling, augmented as I go. All
the way to the far northeast quadrant, a semicircle surround-
ing the sundial where two small stone figures hold open a
book to inscribe the sun's progress. Yards away, a garden of
wild, rambler rosebushes that flourish into winter. This is
the juggler's spot. Often I'd watch him kick a dropped ball
back up into his busy hands. But today someone else is in
possession, the flute player, no less animated, short man in
a vest and cap, shrilling the air like hungry winter birds. His
supple breath, the shiny silver needle of the flute to his lips.
I listen as if I hear my name. Clashing sounds splinter the
air, a red bird's worth of agitation, that or the sharpening
thorns of roses.

Causeway

We were following the usual route up into the hills, the road along the river instructed by the river's path, the one we knew, had always taken to the cabin in the woods, when suddenly he swerved out and found a tree-lined connector road to another way entirely. This one, wide and empty, formed of perfectly joisted pale pine. Custom-made hardwood flooring you could feel in your stockinged feet or even barefoot slip over, it was that smooth, with the scent of shavings, the faint dust of new pale wood. And though inviting, the surface didn't have the depth and steadiness of tarmac. I could tell the car liked its evenness but from time to time shimmied with the shifting sound automobiles make over a protective metal plate on the road before regaining their balance. And out of a wooden, unused silence, I thanked him, congratulated him on having found this utterly appropriate, alternative highway where the warm sky hugged us and the flash of a stream led the way on the left. We went for miles, quieted again, no other car in sight. Once we stopped to make love and later pulled over to the side to cleanse ourselves in the stream where it widened. That single-point perspective, red triangle tip of the sun amid the dense cluster of firs. And all along, the slick of the stream, color thickening to jade.

The Old Playground

Invisible, I'm convinced, I follow the two women, two mothers of the bride, planning their daughters' weddings, overhear them deciding on flowers and music. The upshot, the table arrangements should be no higher than eight inches and centered so the guests can meet one another's eyes. The music, muted, maybe a cello and violin duo from the local Institute, Schubert would be nice, so as not to detract from the ongoing ceremony. Short, straight ginger hair shingles both women's foreheads. They carry their own marriages with them like weighted packs, lending them substance as they step deep into the clayey soil, sucked down by their fashionable boots. It's the playground on Tenth St., built too late for my use, though I still enjoy seeing other little children forming groups and staring up at the sun or kicking a ball around. Black spear-shaped stakes fence off the block-long square. I follow the women's labored progress, but from outside. I can't get in though I am only a wraith and should be able to pass through the bars easily as smoke. The grass rises and sways, buoyed up I fear by hidden colonies of mice. A small pavilion lies far into the interior and I spot some movement. Out of the rich green jumble of pampas grass, the winning, yearning face of a white monkey, a snow monkey. Then as suddenly, it's no longer alone, coupled with another. The pair, side by side, companionable and alert, as if ready to repeat their vows, their shiny, moist puppy eyes looking seriously out at me, over upturned wide, smiling mouths.

Anticipation

We must visit them, they're old, I said. And we did that very night. We walked through the dark garden among the flowering bushes that clung to their house. We saw them in the front window, her arms bare as in summertime, he in a black turtleneck. They were moving furniture around the living room and we saw them again from another window at the side in the kitchen light. L rang the bell and we sat with them in the living room. Their faces so full and young, rosy, looking almost made-up. They didn't have a lot of time they explained. They were waiting for someone and had to go with him to a party where they were expected. They might be able to take us with but if not there were many lovely hotels in the neighborhood. The Windsor, the Exeter, new and shiny facades along the dim streets with big-city glamour. So we waited with them on the comfortable striped couches they had just turned to face one another, maybe for our sakes, in the soft lamplight of the living room. And the man came soon to pick them up, amiable, gray-haired, laughing easily. They left with him and we followed, glad for this short but pleasant visit. They led us to the street of hotels and we entered one, the Exeter, I think. It was noisy and the waiter didn't hear my order so I had to repeat myself, two glasses, and he poured them half-full, maybe it was half-empty. And my friend was there with me and we sat at a table with our Merlot. I turned to look for L. The back of the lobby was lined with pews and people, pale, old people, who sat and keened on the dark wood benches, so I said to myself, let me out of here and got up to look for L, by now my friend, mysteriously gone. I found him and brought him down front to the cocktail tables, by then all filled. At last I stumbled upon a wooden chair, the class-room kind, and another at a small table just off the bandstand where musicians maybe sat out a break. The band was still in place though silent, instruments beside them or at their feet on the small, crowded stage. There was an almost electric din of conversation in the air, maybe anticipatory, or the after-resonance of music.

4. RINSE

Lemon Seller

At the gates to the suk
the lemon seller sits cross-legged
above his wares, above the baskets
of yellow fists. In that rich, dark place
like an opening into the earth.

Blue and purple, his robes.
The Bible calls these colors
the work of cunning men. Around his head,
the endless wrap of a turban.

Earlier, we'd let the train
knot the villages together,
a sequence the desert divided in such
a haphazard way. Soon night rushed up
to cover everything. The train shook so
as we slept that the top came loose
from a fountain pen in my purse.

Where we got off, bands of children
thick around us, were calling out
for coins. How well did I know you then?
You were amused. You devised
an experiment: to keep a pet,
even a child you'd never touch.
You would not be outwardly cruel,
causing it harm, only withhold

partiality. Even now the lemon seller
turns to us from his deep blue cocoon.
The lemons gleam in the sweltering glare
in tight, shiny skins,
in their beautiful balance.

In Here

I can't. I couldn't
go, no
not out there, outside,
with the dim
light on always.

The blinds click
like needles
knitting something
to close me off.

Over the month
I watch the moon
keep its appointments,
the sky hanging down
as it does, to the ground.

Some days I listen
as trees shake the rain
from their shoulders

as the room spins
under the ceiling fan
or the bright sun of day
snaps on and off.

Life Is Real Estate

In a dozen years
I lived in a dozen
different places then in one room
where the bed was lofted
10 feet closer to the ceiling
for the next nine

moving at last
into a big house
around the corner
when I married (even before)
with the weekend annex
of a cabin in the woods
two hours away

where chipmunks chattered
unburrowing, and hunters
locked sacred deer
in their sights,
and from the deck
I could turn my back
on 20 acres of what used
to be a Christmas tree farm.

A birdhouse
the shape of an acorn
hung on a deciduous tree
(of which
there were many,

30 feet high, separated
by a thin crack of sunlight.
They crowned the hill in autumn.)

a house no bird
had ever occupied. Only
an acrobatic family
of flying squirrels
that glided out of the hole in front
one by one to a nearby branch
like a cuckoo when
the hour strikes.

In our cabin
so little came between
inside and out
just wide, thin glass
that cardinals
flung themselves at
mistaking it for air.

Each summer
dames rocket unfurled
and spread
its purple gauze
over the hillside.

Wild turkeys called
like a banner headline
at nightfall, boosting themselves
up into the lowest branches
and were gone
before we woke

and at the end
when we left
we had to leave
all we couldn't
take back with us
into our weekday lives.

Where to Look

I am in the world, lost
to nature. I am in a web of people. They
are my markers, or the jade fingers
of a plant in a window well that I examine
with my fingers, soft as an earlobe.

Where are the small wild things,
shells, stones, to scratch my hands?
I miss the outside birds,
in flight or strutting and perishing.

Even their far-off call, what meaning
here can I attach to it? Where now
do I go to look, to see? To dig deep
until the ground moistens my fingers?
I miss the pines, the house that grows old
among them, sheltering nesting birds in its eaves.

There I'm sure my feet still
fit the ground. Isn't that how you connect
to the earth? Following the fox,
its narrow path through scrub to light.
But the hill has grown too high, too steep
to climb. I would like to draw it down beside me,
be able to pull myself up over it.

2nd Grade

One day I'll come upon you by a bridge in Florida where a manatee is crouching under its mantel of chip bags, assorted plastics, smashed cups. Or in the nearby mom-and-pop beside the bridge. There will be that fine yellow line of light bisecting your eyes that are black as bitter coffee, lips lifted at the corners, sipping nothing but a smile. And it will be like 2nd grade, wondering what you meant, having thought of it deeply all these years.

Early Habit

Sweet sucked
between my teeth

candy cigarettes brought home
in the paper bag from the store
clacking one against another
like sticks of chalk

and was the red end fire
or a lipstick kiss?

On Not Playing the Piano

Susie did. Her family
might have been a band.
A brother clapped his legs
around the cello, and there was
phlegmatic Uncle Ed,
able to make the violin cry.

Ah, but the piano.
So sensual, so powerful,
the rhythmic holding down
of keys to make a music
of your own. "The expense,"
my mother said, and "Like always,
you'll lose interest."

In assembly each morning
someone played, an easy piece
or crossing hands, even a sonata.
I watched their fingers fall
like rain. Was there anything

I wanted more? While Susie,
found to have perfect pitch,
was Gretel in the opera
by Humperdinck, the rest of us
stepped foot to foot, a chorus
of gingerbread children.

I had to content myself
with a harmonica. I blew
into each tiny hole

a clear, true note
though somehow never knew
to join them in a tune.

17

Was it a joke, a disguise
to join the typing pool?
This couldn't have been my life.

It must have been
my mother's then, living
her own again through me,
secretarial school,
the boss she dreamed I'd find
to marry.

Cylinders piled up
on my desk for the machine
that came to life with words,
not like the radio—whose silence
you can't bear when it turns off—
this was just the opposite.

There'd be a gurgle
when I pressed the switch
like the guts churning in my body.
I never could keep up,
let other women with empty hands
come to my rescue. The man
I knew, not really,

through his voice, the handsome boss,
perched a buttock on the corner
of my desk. Later we'd dance
in a white pavilion on a lake
of swans. So I let myself dream

but he dropped me home
with bruises on my arms
and a torn dress.

Rome, 1969

I worked, as long as they'd keep me,
and I prayed they would, an ancient Royal
with its stadium banks of keys my fingers
could not easily push to the bed of letters

at an office beneath the Spanish Steps.
I processed passing Soviet refugees
to freedom with nods and smiles and
a smattering of college Russian.

My husband, sick when we left the States
had only grown sicker. But here we were
calling one of the Seven Hills home,
a tract of umbrella pines opening around us.

Evenings from the balcony we strained
our eyes toward the rich stew of dusk below.
The blond landlady had a glamourous,
improbable name, Signora Grazia della Stella,

our only furniture, cots carted home
from Standa. Mornings from the piazza
I took a bus redolent of perfume and pomade,
and when I took it home at night, of armpits.

(I made my contribution.) Daily, I felt
myself slipping—as when you stand at the edge
of ocean and let the returning waves each time
drag a little more sand out from under you—

and I thought of Keats in his house
midway up the Spanish Steps.
That like him, we wished to be here
so much, we'd be willing to die for it.

Rinse

I watched a friend once
washing a tuna can
under the kitchen faucet
and wondered
was she thinking
maybe if she did it better
he wouldn't leave?

She knew
you were supposed to rinse
the lid of the can
and if she forgot
and had started to open it
with the can opener first
should she keep on,
maybe rinse the tuna
under her hands
to get rid of salt and impurities,
of plastic shreds that sift
to the bottom of the ocean?

How deep should a washing go?
In other words
when should you stop
and couldn't you end up
with nothing left?

Berthe Morisot

She painted, brush in one hand,
solvent in the other.

What she sought, smoke and ghosts
the forgotten
gauzy weight of butterflies.

Women at toilette. Blind curtains
or swell of white underskirts,
the body's curtain.

A cherry tree, petals transparent
as eyelids. Pale dress
of the cherry picker
who vanishes in a cloud.

Painted Ladies

The Painted Lady caterpillar
sheds its skin five times,
like a stripper sloughing off
one layer at a time, to become
what she is meant to be.
Five instars, the wanton dance
to butterfly, in sun or fountains
of rain, ephemeral to eternal.

Like a wet bag of fruit
at last the caterpillar body sags
from its branch and splits.
Two working feelers, the proboscis,
synchronize and long legs unfurl
and open like a safety pin.
The whole body contracts
to move the dazzling wings,
the motion of a flirt,
mobile and erratic,
engaging and avoiding predators.

Haste is the key to the butterfly's
pace. Yet in mating
two join at the abdomen
facing away from each other
which might go on for hours
the way some people do, devotees
of the Kama Sutra, then say goodbye.

Afterward they ride the wind,
a million insects do,
the Arctic to Morocco using
the radar of the sun, 9,000 miles.
But always they return to Africa,
the Spanish scientist awaiting
them. With a finger he'll
lightly graze the outer edge
of tired wings of the old, arriving,
dying butterflies, setting up
to capture them, and then
a gentle shake of net, let them go.

Mushrooms

Admire mushrooms.
They hide and know
just when
to come out.

Puff! Like me, an accident,
there I was, maybe
never meant to be.

And mushrooms are nearly
beyond description, since
only 6% have ever been
described

all Primary Process,
what the mind only thinks
and doesn't yet have a name for.

They remind me
of what we don't know
about ourselves,
feelings that are kept
underground and seem
connected to nothing else.

Heedlessly, mushrooms
come between things,
join algae
for what they can use,
sugars to make lichens,
grinding rock to soil.

Mushrooms thumb
a ride up into air.
In fact, if air had a crust
it would be a mushroom.

Deer

The deer at Nara
so quietly surround you
in hope, no, expectation
of the deer cookies
you buy for something like a dollar,
trust never in doubt.

Last week at the sides
of the Expressway
I counted seven fallen deer
alongside jettisoned sofas
and mattresses. Had they leapt
from the ice-bearded cliffs
mute into traffic?

Like the voiceless rabbit
crossing the road near the end
of my first marriage. In the I-Ching
I had that day flipped
to the hexagram:
Abandoning the carriage.

Dark night
and a turnoff through woods.
We swerved too late to stop,
though I cried out, another rabbit,
maybe the second of the pair,
already under the wheels.

Lee Morgan

Jazz. That was the music got me
through my teens. Dizzy hired Morgan,
what his wife too called him, at 18,
skinny kid almost as good as him
who wore clothes well.

                    He'd be
Helen's husband but he could
have been her son. I liked her voice,
only the one interview 20 years after
getting out of jail. She spoke
like Billie Holiday, the squeak and lilt.

What she did best
was to cook. Always a big pot
of beans on the stove, musicians needed
to eat, not stagger
onto the bandstand drunk.

She worked a switchboard days,
big Afro like Angela, song named for
Angela Davis he later played.

For years he'd shot up heroin, lost his teeth,
came to gigs in slippers,
"They're comfortable."
The others knew he'd hocked his shoes.

It's always winter in this story.
He, in a little jacket
when they met,

so Helen had gone out to buy a coat.
She got him clean on Methadone,
made deals like she was his manager,
even carried his case.

"I'll be your woman, not your main woman,"
she said. But someone else
had come with him to Slug's.
He was playing with the quintet
he formed, sure it would last forever.

A Nor'easter, two feet of snow that night.
When he tried to get Helen to leave,
a gun tumbled out of her purse.
The ambulance took over an hour.
"Could I have done this?" She as surprised
as anyone. She wished she would
have shot herself.

5. SPIN

What I Saw What Was Said What I Heard

I look out back for the moon
but it's always in a different place.

*

Yards like empty boxes,
overhead view of a Japanese
painting.

*

On the street next day
last of the trash:
white satin slipper that said "Bride."

*

Unclear what my friend was telling me,
what I heard.
Elgar, octet? Motet?
Elgar, allegro? A chorus
singing it or humming.

*

Tai chi, the substitute explained, is like
silk reeling. For years
from my usual teacher
I heard "silk feeling." Now suddenly
it made sense.

*

Winter. Clouds and smoke.
In the night, visitations,
mysterious shadows.

Then the house heaves
with moans of children at the door.

*

A woman I know organizes
group hums—
she studied with Meredith Monk.
On Google she can pinpoint
each participant anywhere in the world.
Someone, each one, voices a breath
and holds it.

Awaited Storm

The air is still, the sky holds
its breath.
A man in a wool cap,
a dog. I'm thinking, Heade,
Heade's *Approaching Thunder Storm*.

Wide, flat canvas
rain cloud the length
of the horizon. Yellow-blue sky,
a red checkmark of lightning.
Someone fast rowing in
from a moored sailboat.

It's the careful reconstruction
of a late-summer day,
light pressed out of the sky,
canvas painted shut.

While here the hurricane
has come to us
and the winds,
before the dark blot of night.

"Lie down," he says,
"beside me." And the thunder
that is the lightning's voice,
rolls through like a train.

Saint-Saëns
on the radio. So there is
music too in the room

deviating from words, from silence,
notes drawn up into the storm.

Green summer
sways at the window.

And as if acknowledging
the end of day, night
before the night, we lie down
together. Nobody to tuck us in.
Who else would know the rules?

Non-Fungible Tokens

music from another room

one narrow flower stopped by a vase

until petals shake loose

a glancing kiss

the brush of elbows along a stair

a space left open in the body

the unquiet sea

imagining its way to the door

this ship of ours—

who is pilot then

who, passenger?

Crumpled Paper Theory

Do they count the creases
or the flat areas in between,
facets formed, like the facets
of a diamond that let in light?

It turns out they measure
the "crease network,"
lengths that somehow add up
each time to a similar
though slightly different number.

The Israeli scientists call it
"Kvetching" the paper.
They don't mean make it
complain, make it say "Uncle."
But squeeze, press it. For crumpled,

paper squeezes together
like the body in pain.
And before there was paper,
what was to be crumpled besides
the beautiful, ruinous earth?

Look at eroding rockpiles,
pebble beaches. The way
ground crumples into mountains
and valleys along the seam of rivers.

And how much mileage can you get
out of a single piece of paper?

It's known as claustrophobia
what the paper goes through,
geometric frustration
which has to be relieved
by uncrumpling.

It's a theory I like because
you know you can never be exact.
I have always been careless
of dates and times, letting things slip by
but I see how maybe it doesn't matter.

In fact, I could crumple a day,
a single page from the calendar,
and let it straighten as much
as it wants and have it still.

I'd get a sheet of paper back
mussed, for sure, though now
it would be paper with a history.

Magical Thinking

It was a book about grief
I'd put on hold at the library
so it had passed through many hands
by the time it reached mine
about a husband and daughter
both dead in the same year
by an author I trusted who hadn't
written much thereafter

as if she couldn't think
of more to say, though the book
came to me many wars and deaths—
9/11, for instance—later,
and when it fell once from hands
shaking with my own losses
and split open, I found a drop of blood
smeared along a page and knew
I couldn't read in it any longer.

Bitter Herb

the lettuce
its rough surface, its tang
and leathery leaf

the blessings that come to us
the blessings that pass us by

the tiny flame that's lit
in the house
the house always ready

the hunger the sorrow
the narrowing door

Beginning Light

and the birds are scrambling
over who gets first say

while people who sleep rough
on the ground, do they stir
at the encouragement of morning?

I think of my brothers
praying on rising each day
of their lives thus far,

did they extract phylacteries
from the velvet pouch in a drawer

did they remember
in the forgetting wards
of nursing homes to give thanks

for the next day and the next,
strapping themselves to God
in hard leather bands?

Cloth House

The tent blisters like a flap of skin
in wind. Not a house, not solid
geometry. Limp isosceles, wings
fastened to the grass that fringes
the azalea garden. It doesn't
accommodate your height, or only
at a single central point.
But some solace anyway, shedding
elements and disapproving looks.

The good thing is how it can
be carried along, collapsed, and
be reconstituted. How portable it is
folded on your shoulders. You could
almost wear it like a turtle
his or her exoskeleton though it wouldn't
provide the same level of protection.

And because it is not grafted on,
someone might make off with it. And
afterward, where would you be?
What does it really offer beside
relief from prying eyes as you sleep,
or rain? The worst is how easily
authorities can plow it down
where it isn't wanted, and
wouldn't that be anywhere? Whisked away
and then you're homeless as ever.

After Tarkovsky, *Andrei Rublev*

—for Bill Kulik

So that was Russian film, pellucid as any,
penetrated by light like brushstrokes
or memory. Translucent folds of saints' robes,
the painted icon of three Marys that fades
to three frolicking green horses on a spit
of land. And in that dark time when holiness
on a wall was all that held off wars
or weather in the long middle ages.

"Verstunkene tunder!" I once heard a little
Irish boy cry out from the safety of a car
in rain. He, just come from a year spent
in Germany with his parents. Outside,
floods, the precarity of horses. He had to be cold.
I didn't think to slip over him my thin jacket
as the driver, herself a mother, did.

Old friend, I will never get to say to you,
again, after the long winter of that film,
words we learned much of a lifetime ago,
Russian words I remember to this day.
Verbs, mainly, from a Volga German professor
who would later teach me whatever I know
of German too, sweet man with a lisp of no

decided national identity. Beside me
the boy I would marry, we two sitting
on one side of the aisle, and just across,
you, with the acuity of Ukrainian ancestors,
blond crewcut, perfect pronunciation:

I listen
I speak
I must
I work
I love
I don't know,
enough to live a short life in another place.
The little song about snow on the Neva,
a child's song, for we are children
in that language and I for one will never
get any older in it.

        We two, just friends,
I'd say, though no one would believe me. *Drug v druge,*
I wrote on the label of his birthday wine
in that early time. You, it turns out, I knew
far longer though not so well. I, now, the only
one left watching in the black and white
that blooms into color like real life.

Procession

Start by picking up the chair
you must wear on your shoulders.

Position yourself. Turn one way or the other
when you have decided who will sit in it.

It will always be too heavy
even if it's only that slight young woman before
the vacant store

in her white nightdress
asleep on a bedsheet wet with rain
that causes the crowd to swerve.

Someone has left her a sandwich wrapped in cellophane
for when the spell is lifted.

Or maybe you are remembering another more solitary time
when the bus got to the brick side of the bank

or you came up gritty gum-stuck stairs
from the subway

eyes rising slowly
to the white-silled windows set into the brick—

a leftover moon melting into day,
or you could hear the tick of rain.

You are not sure what you might have been doing there.

You forget anything
you no longer have a use for.

Street Voice

Mr. Melon
lived between two other little girls
Naomi and Tess
two loves two profound hungers
factory nights imagining them, and in the day he was free
to mind on his lap one or the other
while a mother went to the store.

Away too his Irish wife
her squandered laughter
her black hair that fell like the pelt of an animal
along her shoulders.

We lived in white rows
like a piano
if your finger pressed a key
a low moan would escape
or a vault of secrets open
and that was someone else's house.

I went through the alley
to play Monopoly at Arthur's,
Oren in his wheelchair already seated
and if I was lucky Arthur's father
home from work before I left, handsome face
with its grown-up, grown-in 5 o'clock shadow.

My mother made me a birthday party only the once
when I was seven
everyone sat around our long dining room table.
I wouldn't look up from my plate

though they had brought little games
where beads fell into holes in a picture,
and coloring books from the 5 & dime.

On the next block one day a dead thing lay
like a discarded red ribbon
a mouse I thought but I didn't know
what a mouse looked like, thought no
when I saw the feathers
a tiny unfinished bird
fallen from its nest skinny legs spilling out.

Beach Dreaming

So long since I've been, my colorless skin can't remember a tan. And this, a narrow, cramped beach, not very pretty. Spoiled water sluices out of a conduit far up and dampens the sand, all along threaded with tangles of seaweed as after a storm, dark red and green like mermaid hair, sleek in my fingers with bumps I'd squeeze before there was bubble wrap. But it's my beach, the one I've dreamt into being where I'm happy to find myself, watching the ocean flow in all its unexpected directions. I have to tear myself away, look for my path back along high curbs I skipped over, coming. Block after block where trees lead me, evenly spaced before houses. A man on a bike passes, his plaid shirtsleeves rolled up to the elbow, but it isn't you. At last in the held back light of dusk I come to a narrow, quiet street, drenched in white blossoms and another man in a plaid shirt on a bike right where our house should be, but he isn't you either.

ACKNOWLEDGMENTS

The Laurel Review—"Tan Espadrilles," "Monkfish, Manatee," "Mirror"

The Alaska Quarterly Review—"Mom-in-a-Box"

Storm Cellar—"Peace"

MacQueen's Quinterly—"Angel, Sleep," "Before the Trip"

CCAR Journal— "*Er Lakht*," "Beginning Light"

Porter Gulch Review—"Cloth House"

Valley Voices—"The Lemon Seller" (as "In Cairo"), "Short Memoirs of Life on Earth"

Moonstone Press: 25th Anniversary Poetry Ink Anthology (vol. 2)—"Case"; *Virus Anthology*—"In Here"; *Featured Poets Anthology, 2021*—"Deer"

The Diamond Cutter's Daughter: A Poet's Memoir—"Laugh Track"

NOTES

The book in "Magical Thinking" is Joan Didion's *The Year of Magical Thinking*

"Painted Ladies" was inspired by a 2016 Nature documentary, *The Great Butterfly Adventure*, directed by Adrian Cale

"Lee Morgan" is based on the documentary, *I Called Him Morgan,* directed by Kasper Collins

"Short Memoirs of Life on Earth" was written for my friend Larry Stier's 70th birthday

"Case" is based on the ballet *Come Out* by Anne Teresa de Keersmaeker, music by Steve Reich, where I learned Daniel Hamm's story

"Rome, 1969." Jews in that year were for the first time permitted to leave the USSR, facilitated by the agency HIAS, to seek asylum in other countries

I am grateful to John Zheng, editor of *Valley Voices*, for a comprehensive interview in the Spring, 2022 issue and for publishing my poems over the years

Thanks too to Larry Robin of Moonstone Press and the Moonstone Arts Center for many readings and inclusion in anthologies

My gratitude to Jeanne Murray Walker and Sharon White for their suggestions on various poems and to Elizabeth Murphy at Grid Books, also a poet, for her caring and careful editing

ELAINE TERRANOVA has published seven collections of poems, including *Dollhouse*, which won the 2013 Off the Grid Poetry Prize, and most recently, *Perdido*. Her poems and prose have appeared in a number of literary magazines and anthologies and her translation of Euripides' *Iphigenia at Aulis* was published by the Penn Greek Drama Series. Her awards include grants from the Pennsylvania Council on the Arts, the Walt Whitman Award, NEA and Pew fellowships, and a Pushcart Prize. In 2021, her book *The Diamond Cutter's Daughter: A Poet's Memoir* was published.